More About Archie: The Post Puppy Years

By Helen Edwards

DISCLAIMER

The information and recommendations in this book are given without any guarantees on behalf of the author, who disclaims any liability with the use of this material.

To Simon and Archie
xx

Contents

INTRODUCTION

I got my Zuchon puppy, Archie, when he was eight weeks old. I was a first-time puppy parent and I found the experience hard, harder than I'd been expecting, that's for sure. I also became very anxious and that became my motivation for writing my first book, *All About Archie: Bringing Up A Puppy*, because I wanted to try and help other people in the same position.

These days, life with Archie is a lot more relaxed, so much so that I have almost forgotten those difficult first weeks with him (almost, but not quite!). That said, Archie's only three, so he's young and full of energy and keeps me and my husband, Simon, on our toes.

Even when your puppy's grown the worrying doesn't end. When Archie's sick, I have to do my best not to catastrophise and imagine the worst. Going on holiday, I worry he's going to think we've abandoned him when we drop him off at the pet-sitters. I wonder sometimes if we're doing enough for him, and a newer fear is that someone's going to try to steal him. It's all a matter of getting things into proportion.

Your life does change with a dog in it. I'm Archie's mum. I know some people will have an issue with me calling myself that – tough! You do, in effect, become a parent to your dog. Archie needs feeding, he needs exercising, he needs grooming, he needs his ears cleaning, he needs the gunk from under his eyes to be removed, he needs his teeth brushing ... He can't do any of these things for himself, and never will be able to. I just get on with things – the way he looks at me or snuggles up to me is all the thanks I need.

I loved writing about Archie in the first book, and now find I have more I can share about life with a young dog. Plus, Archie wants to have more input and, well, he's the boss (or he likes to think he is). I was also thrilled to get some contributions from other puppy and dog owners, because I want to get the message across that dogs (young and old), as much as we love them, are hard work. People

5

need to know that before they make the final decision to get one. Let's start with Rachel and Maisie's story. Enjoy!

Love from Helen and Archie x

Archie: *Humans are hard work too! I think Mum should chillax.*

'The similarities to a baby are uncanny!'

Rachel is mum to young Maisie, who at the time of first writing was twelve weeks old. Maisie is a Retriever/Border Collie mixed breed. She's not only Rachel's first puppy, but her first dog! Rachel's had Maisie since she was nine weeks old. Here she shares her story, along with some tips on being a puppy parent.

Preparation

I did quite a bit of research before getting Maisie. I'd been planning it for about a year. I watched a lot of YouTube videos on training and I also joined a couple of Facebook groups. I read a lot of articles, and I talked to people, trying to absorb as much as possible. I definitely think it helped. It's kind of like before you have your first baby, you're never really prepared. My preparation went a long way in making sure my expectations matched up as closely as possible to reality.

The early days

One thing I'd 'heard', but didn't take in, was how needy puppies are. It's not like a cat that is happy to have some independence. You become mommy. Also, the play biting – wow! It gets very, very irritating. It doesn't usually hurt, but I didn't realise how relentless young puppies get with it. I'm pretty good about immediately redirecting Maisie to a toy, or holding her and putting her in positions that make it difficult to get her mouth around me. I can calm her down, but my kids don't have the same finesse. Maisie's put holes in a few shirts because they try to pull away. I'm really looking forward to Maisie outgrowing this phase.

I've had Maisie for just over a fortnight now. I think we've settled into a sort of crazy new normal. Puppies sleep a lot (they should get 18-20 hours of sleep a day!) so that helps me get things done. Maisie can wake at the drop of a hat, though, so I'm always telling the kids to be quiet if she's asleep. Our morning routine is chaos. Getting the kids' lunches packed, and everyone dressed and ready to catch the bus is a challenge. It's probably one of the most frustrating parts of the day because I really need thirty minutes to focus exclusively on getting us all ready, yet it's also the time when Maisie's full of energy and needs to go poop! I've started insisting that one of the kids takes her out whilst I'm packing lunches.

Every outing takes some thought. How long will I be gone? Is it some place Maisie can come with me? Is there someone who can stay at home with her? I try to save most errands for when someone can be home with her to minimise the time she spends alone in her crate. I usually like being a pretty spontaneous person, taking off to go someplace on a whim, but I can't be like that now.

We also have to have elaborate systems of doors that remain closed, doors that remain open, and gates to ensure that the cats can access their food and litter, but the puppy can't.

A typical day with Maisie
A typical day begins around 7 a.m. It's a toss-up whether my alarm wakes me, or whether it's Maisie whining to come out of her crate. I take her outside to pee, then optimistically try to put her back in the crate to see if she'll sleep a little longer. At the weekends I can sometimes get away with it, but on week days when I have to get up early she never sleeps through that, and gets very upset if I leave her in her crate.

After the kids have left, Maisie's ready to nap. She naps well when the house is quiet so this is the best time for me to shower, do housework, and so on. As soon as she wakes, I take her outside again. And as long as she's awake, I try to take her outside at least hourly. We mostly hang around at home so the middle of the day is relatively chilled. My four-year-old is home too, so we might play outside, or play with some toys inside.

Maisie loves a natural chew (like bully sticks) so during low energy times, she'll relax and chew. I try to ensure she gets a real good nap in before the kids come home from school because once they're home, she won't nap nearly as well! They get her really riled up. But then they also help with playing with her and taking her outside, so it's nice that that doesn't fall 100 percent to me.

I try and have at least a couple of times during the day where we practise training, or even learn something new. Maisie's great at 'sit' and she'll 'come' sometimes. We're practising 'leave it', which she does pretty well when we're playing (she knows she'll get a treat if she waits a few seconds), but that doesn't yet translate to other situations. Something new we're practicing is impulse control. Before something she's highly anticipating, like coming out of her crate, I ask her to sit and remain in that position while I open the door. She shouldn't exit the crate until she's given permission. It's hard for her, but she's slowly getting it! It's such an important skill, to have that kind of impulse control. It will lay a good foundation for getting her to obey during other times of high excitement.

I put Maisie to bed at around 9 p.m., usually right after I put my kids to bed. I take her for one last toilet break, then she goes into her crate. I lie on my bed next to her crate until she's asleep, then I sneak out.

Three months later …
Maisie is now six months old. Things have settled down, but of course new things arise to keep things interesting. Maisie sleeps through the night, and I now get to sleep in on the weekends. I'm a night owl, but I put her to bed with the kids and wake her to take her out one last time before I go to bed. The play biting has mostly stopped. Maisie doesn't really try to mouth on me anymore, but she'll still go after the kids, just not as bad as before. I try to explain to the kids that their

body language and reactions invite her to keep biting, but they don't get it. They seem to think it's funny.

Maisie learnt about counter surfing a couple months ago, which is highly frustrating and difficult to train because every time she does it, it's like she gets a reward and reinforces the behaviour. I've learned to be very, very careful and not leave food unattended on any surface for even a second. Dishes get picked up immediately. It's getting better – I think all my precautions have gotten her out of the habit of constantly looking for opportunities to sneak some unauthorised snacks. I don't quite trust her to not take advantage of an opportunity that presents itself though, so more training is needed.

Rachel's tips for puppy parents
Work on training for issues before they come up. If you have a medium/large breed of dog, start getting in the habit of obsessively keeping all food out of reach before they get big enough to reach the counters. It's way easier to train before they've had a taste of forbidden fruit.

Maisie then and now

Photographs © Rachel Radtke

'Just like children, puppies and dogs are likely to be more interested in the packaging than the contents.'

HAPPY DOG

Dogs can't read a book or watch a TV programme like humans can, and yet they need mental stimulation. A walk can be mentally stimulating, providing your dog's allowed to sniff to his heart's content, and more stimulation can be got from games, training, chews, and puzzle toys. Here are some ideas to enrich your dog's day:

A New Trick

Assuming your puppy or dog can do all the basics like 'sit' and so on, why not teach him something new? I decided to teach Archie how to shake paws/hands. The way I did it was to take one of his front paws in my hand, shake it, then give him a treat immediately afterwards. I later introduced the word 'shake'. Now I simply hold my hand out and say 'shake' and he lifts his paw for me.

Archie: *I lift my paw up even when I haven't been asked to nowadays. It's worth a try! And Mum says I look very cute when I do it.*

I've also taught Archie the word 'finished'. It's handy because I use it for times like when I've finished grooming him (he knows he can relax), or when he's had the last of his treats (he knows not to look for any more and he settles).

Antler

We've yet to find a chew which Archie enjoys for lengthy sessions like some dogs do, but he does like chewing on an antler from time to time. I read some reports that dogs can break their teeth on too hard a chew, antlers included, which concerned me. I thought about throwing Archie's antler away, but as he doesn't gnaw on it for lengthy periods – he mostly enjoys licking peanut butter off it – I decided to keep it. He's never left alone with it. And I've recently bought him a half antler chew, which is softer.

Not all antlers are the same. I tried Archie with a few different brands until we discovered Green & Wilds. Their antlers are 100 percent natural, hypoallergenic, they last for ages, and they provide your dog with minerals, having been produced from naturally shed antlers (the deer are free ranging). Archie loves his.

Balls

I bought Archie one of those footballs – the lightweight kind designed for young kids. Some dogs, even small dogs, enjoying pushing such a ball around. Not Archie. He didn't show the slightest bit of interest. He prefers Kong tennis balls, the mini variety. He absolutely loves it when we have two on the go – he tries his best to get both of them in his mouth, but can't!

Did you know you can get dog toys which flash? Archie's got a ball. It's more for outside use, but we have occasionally switched some of the lights off in the evening and played fetch with Archie using the ball. It's just something different to do; it mixes things up a bit for your dog.

Buster Activity Mat

I bought the Buster Activity Mat starter kit for Archie, which consists of the mat itself and three puzzles, along with a bag to store everything in. I also bought him another puzzle to go with it – a book.

Each puzzle has different levels of difficulty, so give your puppy or dog the greatest chance of success by starting off on level one, and only when they've got used to that should you move to level two. It will keep things interesting for your dog. For example, with the book puzzle you begin simply by attaching it to the mat using the press studs. Then put one treat in one of the 'pages' and let your dog find it. Then increase the number of pages you put treats into.

I introduced the puzzles to Archie slowly, as I didn't want to overwhelm him. The set includes an envelope, water lily and a cone cloth. I tend to get the mat out in the evening, and put a little kibble in there, or even some raw carrot, which Archie loves!

Kong Quest Wishbone
Archie has a Kong Quest Wishbone, which I stuff with kibble or treats, and I also add some paste, and it keeps him busy for a while. It's made out of a synthetic material, so it doesn't smell, unlike the Kong classic. Archie was never keen on his red Kong classic, and I have a theory that it was because it had a strong rubbery smell, which no amount of washing could remove.

Lickimat
Lickimats are basically rubber-type mats with a textured surface upon which you can spread all sorts of things for your dog to lick off.

Archie loves his Lickimat. So far I have put plain yoghurt on it, peanut butter, Kong paste, and Archie's wet food (but not all at once!). I tend to leave most of his wet food in a pile so it's easy for him to eat, and just spread a bit of it into the mat. I don't want to frustrate him as this is his main meal we're talking about. These mats are difficult to clean, but that's just a little grumble; I'm still glad I got one for Archie. There are three versions, each with a different surface. I bought Archie's from Amazon.

PickPocket Fabric Food Foragers
There's a crate and a mat version, and they come in different sizes. They basically encourage nose work, working on a dog's sense of smell to root out treats, kibble – anything you put in the pockets. They come in different sizes. I got both versions. The floor mat was a success straightaway. I didn't need to show Archie what to do as we'd done nose work before. His snout was straight in there, finding treats.

The crate version has ties to secure it to a crate. Again, Archie picked it up quickly. I highly recommend them – they're washable too!

Puzzle Ball
Because Archie doesn't seem to like strongly scented rubber toys, whenever I want to buy him a more durable toy, I look for ones made out of thermoplastic (TPR). They are non-toxic and hard-wearing. Archie's got a puzzle ball made out of TPR and he loves it. So if your dog doesn't take to the Kong classic, try an alternative puzzle toy, and maybe consider ones made out of TPR.

Snuffle Mats
Snuffle mats seem to be all the rage for dogs at the moment. A snuffle mat consists of strips of fleece tied onto a rubber mat with holes in it, the idea being to hide treats or kibble amongst the fleece for your dog to sniff out. You can buy them online, but there are a lot of DIY versions.

Because I enjoy making things I decided to make one for Archie. I followed the instructions from a tutorial I found online (see the Useful Links at the end of this book). I had some old fleece blankets I was able to make use of. The only thing I had to buy was the rubber sink mat, so it didn't cost much.

It took me a while to make, but only because I worked on a small section at a time. I found it quite therapeutic threading the strips through and tying them in knots (enrichment for humans!). As to whether Master Archie liked it – he did.

I don't put all of Archie's puzzle toys out at once – I alternate them each day in a bid to keep things fresh for him.

Walkies
I've realised more and more that the walk is Archie's walk – if he wants to spend it sniffing, then who am I to drag him

away from the leaf that is providing so much interest? Dogs have different ideas about walks than we humans do, so I'm trying to be more relaxed about it and let Archie go at his own pace, and sniff to his heart's content. I also take treats with me and throw them from time to time for Archie to 'go find' (I check the verge for poo first!). It makes me so happy to see Archie's tail wagging. Imagine if you could somehow harness the energy of wagging tails.

Enrichment For Free
Puzzle toys can cost a lot of money, but there are lots of ways to entertain your dog for free. When Archie was a puppy I used an old baking tray (for making fairy cakes) and put kibble inside, placing a ball on top of each one. Archie had to move the balls aside to claim his prize. I also used to hide treats in one of his blankets, which I folded up, leaving him to seek them out.

You could roll up treats in a towel, hide them in your dog's basket or den, leave a trail round the house for him to follow – the possibilities are endless. I don't leave Archie alone with towels because he has a tendency to chew them, so when he's found all the treats I put the towel away until the next time.

If you've just received a delivery, why not fill the empty box with toys and treats for your dog to seek out? A word of caution: if your dog is likely to chew the cardboard don't leave him alone with it. Supervise the activity and then put the box away until the next time.

I throw some treats for Archie to search for in the garden. Another thing I do is put some treats in Archie's paddling pool. Let me explain. I bought a paddling pool for Archie during the summer, but he wouldn't go in the water. We later placed it indoors and put all his toys in it. It's working as a kind of play area. Archie's started to put his toys back in there, so he's learning what 'tidy' means!

For more ideas on how to entertain your dog, I recommend joining the Canine Enrichment group on Facebook (see Useful Links).

Archie: *I LOVE, LOVE, LOVE to sniff. It's my absolute favourite thing to do.*

'I personally found having a new baby was easier than a puppy!'

Bryony Yates is mum to six-month-old Luna, a Whippet/Sprocker mixed breed, who was seven weeks old when Bryony took her home. Luna isn't the first puppy Bryony has had – she's had two other dogs in the past – but I think it's fair to say that Luna has proved to be the most challenging. Here Bryony shares her views on being a puppy parent.

I did lots of research into all the breeds, Whippet, Springer and Cocker, and I think it helped me to understand Luna more. That said, the early days with her were horrible. She would bite all the time and snatch things. We had to watch her 100 percent of the time – it was exhausting. I felt as though I had lost my life. I couldn't even clean the house because that would have meant leaving Luna to play by herself, and I couldn't trust her not to eat something or have an accident, which I would need to clean up. We did have a crate for her, but she would scream and cry so loud when she was in it, so putting her in that wasn't an option initially. I literally had to be with her ALL the time. I felt trapped with this horrible little pooping, snappy, shark thing with needle-sharp teeth that ripped skin and clothes … it broke me. For the first three weeks I just cried – I regretted getting her.

To people thinking about getting a new puppy I would say this: be prepared for your whole life to change. Puppies are really, really hard work. And to new puppy owners I would advise finding puppy classes to help with training and bonding. Don't give up because things do get better. Luna is now six months old and she's a dream dog. We love her to bits. She has settled down, she is trained, and I can leave her to play whilst I get on with things. Life is thankfully much calmer.

Luna then and now

Photographs © Bryony Yates

'Unlike with children, you can't explain to your dog what's happening. You can't ring him for a chat.'

HAPPY HOLIDAYS

Prior to going on our first holiday with Archie, Simon and I were both apprehensive as to how we'd manage away from home, with a dog. Simon was also concerned about the amount of time we'd be in the car. We planned regular stops, but even so, it meant a lot of travelling for Archie.

We were lucky to find some decent dog-friendly self-catering accommodation. Some places have rules where your dog isn't allowed on any of the furniture, so be warned. Other places were more relaxed. I took an extra throw with us to use on the sofa, just in case one wasn't provided. We were always respectful of the accommodation, and left it looking as good (sometimes cleaner!) as it did when we first entered it, and we always got our security deposit back.

I took Archie's bedding, favourite toys, and chews with us, in order to help him adjust by having some familiar things around him. And we bought a small rucksack to keep wipes, gloves and poo bags, along with Archie's water bottle, treats, waterproof coat, and so on; things we needed to be close to hand whilst we were on the move.

The gloves and wipes were for a potential dirty bottom. That happened to us once. We were in town when Archie did a poo, which got stuck (basically it was hanging from his bottom). Our attempts to remove it caused it to smear. It was like doing the walk of shame back to the car!

I found Trip Advisor to be a wonderful resource for finding places to eat where we could take Archie inside. We were travelling during the summer and the weather was fine so there was always the option to sit and eat outside, but sometimes you want to sit inside. I made sure to review everywhere we went, as they were all brilliant places to take your dog and I wanted to spread the word.

Taking Archie on holiday with us makes for a very different sort of holiday. I personally don't think it's as relaxing. You have to plan ahead more; you can't just go wherever you want as not everywhere is dog friendly. You'll have to take it in turns to go into service stations, for example, and one of you will have to wait outside the shop.

Although it's nice to include your dog, think about it from their point of view too: crowds (depending upon where you're going), travelling in the car, a change of routine … If you've got a totally chilled out dog, then that's fine, but in other cases it might be kinder to leave him behind.

Holidays without Archie are now bittersweet. On the plus side, you know that gloomy/sad feeling you get when the holiday is nearly over? For me it's now countered by knowing I'll see Archie when we get home.

It also helps knowing Archie is with someone we trust. For our most recent holiday, although it meant going miles out of our way, we took Archie back to our old pet-sitter, Paula, as we haven't yet managed to find any suitable pet-sitters where we live.

Archie hadn't seen Paula for a while, so rather than take him for a week's break straightaway, we took him to Paula's for a short break to re-acclimatise. I was worried about how he'd be, but as soon as we arrived he was pulling me to Paula's door. It was like old times and he settled in straight away.

It's ideal if you can get your dog used to regular day care, and perhaps short breaks, before leaving them with the pet-sitter for a lengthier period of time. If your dog isn't used to being away from you, and there comes a time when you have to be apart (not just holidays, a hospital stay for example), it's going to be hard on your dog.

Archie was bursting with joy when he saw us waiting at the door for him on our return. It was lovely and I was so proud of him, as Paula said how well he'd settled in and how much she'd miss him. He's so adaptable and is always up for some fun.

Archie says: *It doesn't seem that long before Mum and Dad come to pick me up. I have no idea of the time. Lol. Like Mum tells me, they always come back. I know that. And I love staying with Auntie Paula. I'm having my own holiday, so don't worry about me, Mum!*

Christmas

Despite dog charities doing their best to educate people that Christmas isn't the best time of year to get a puppy (and certainly not to give one as a surprise present), each year there are still people who think it's a great idea. Little thought seems to have gone into what happens after Christmas.

When everything's calmed down, when the tree's been packed away, what of life with a puppy then? Did the recipient really want one? Were they ready for one? Can they afford the upkeep? Parents who bought a puppy for their kids will likely discover that they, not the kids, will be the ones cleaning up after it.

Unlike novelty jumpers or that strange-looking vase your aunt bought you for Christmas, dogs have feelings. Puppies will begin to get used to their new home and to bond with their family, yet all of a sudden are uprooted and taken to a rescue centre, not having a clue what's going on – is that fair?

Puppies are hard work whatever time of year you get one, but Christmas is generally a stressful period of time, so the odds are that a new puppy in the house will be the tipping point.

If you've never had a puppy before and you're thinking of getting one around Christmas, have you thought it through? Your routine is likely to be different. Although puppies will need socialising, they do need a bit of time to settle down. If you're having people round, did you know that you'll need to provide a quiet spot for your puppy to have some time out? Young children will need to be watched so that they don't pester the puppy too much – puppies need lots of sleep. And if you have plans to go out, are you taking your puppy with you or are you leaving him behind? Does he travel well? Will he be welcome at your friend's house? He can't be left on his own for long, so who's going to stay at home with him?

If you work, have you factored in enough time to get your puppy used to his new home before you return to work after Christmas? Who will look after pup then? Have you begun getting him used to being alone for short periods of time?

Maybe you tend to have a quiet Christmas, and your routine doesn't change all that much, so you think you can cope with a puppy. A word of caution; Simon and I brought Archie home in late January 2016 and after an overwhelming couple of weeks with our new puppy, we both said we were glad we didn't get him just before Christmas. If we had, Christmas would have been cancelled! So think about it from that perspective too.

Archie: *When Mum's wrapping Christmas presents I like to 'help' by walking over the paper.*

'There are moments when I could cheerfully kill him.'

KATH AND GATSBY

Kath is mum to one-year-old Zuchon, Gatsby. She's had Gatsby since he was nine weeks old. He's not her first puppy, but he is her first Zuchon. Here Kath shares her views on being a puppy parent.

I did do some research prior to getting Gatsby, but I have since found out that every dog is different. During the early days with Gatsby I was very anxious because he was so small. Puppies are hard work, but I truly believe in nurture not nature. Listen to the advice of other dog owners, but bear in mind that all dogs are different, and have their own little quirks and personalities. You need to adopt a common sense attitude and understand that there is no such thing as a bad dog – perseverance is the key. On the whole, life with Gatsby is perfect and I am absolutely smitten with him – he makes me laugh on a daily basis.

Gatsby then and now

Photographs © Kath Pearce

23

'Food can affect your dog's behaviour, so if you're having any issues with him, it's worth taking another look at what he's eating.'

HEALTHY DOG

When we moved we had to register Archie with a new veterinary practice. I did some research, checked out reviews, and eventually chose one I had a good feeling about.

As a newbie, Archie was given a free health check. Whilst we were there the vet told us about their Lifetime Care Club, for which you pay a certain amount each month depending upon the weight of your dog, and you're then covered for flea and worming treatments, vaccinations, nail clipping, a six month health check, and more. You save money over the course of a year because the vaccinations and flea and worming prevention are discounted. We decided to join and it's working well, so why not enquire whether your veterinary practice runs a similar scheme?

Anal Glands
During a health check, we mentioned that Archie had been scooting more than usual (you know, dragging his bottom along the floor). There was also a fishy smell coming from his bottom area! It turned out he needed his anal glands expressing. These usually clear themselves when a dog goes for a poo, but sometimes intervention is required. It was done within thirty seconds. Archie didn't like it much, but I'm sure he felt better afterwards. And the scooting stopped!

Archie: *No comment!*

First Aid Kit
I bought a first aid kit specifically for pets/dogs. Thankfully I haven't had to use it yet, but it's there just in case. For further advice on first aid for dogs check out the Blue Cross for Pets website (see Useful Links).

Medication

Keep medication, both yours and your dog's, far out of reach. Some human tablets, like ibuprofen, are coated in sugar which your dog could take a fancy to. And as tablets for dogs are often flavoured these days, your dog could be tempted to eat the whole packet if he can get hold of it!

More About Food

Some people say raw is best, others swear by kibble. Others feed their dog wet food, or a mixture of wet and dry. Some give their dog human food. I personally didn't want to be dealing with raw food, and you have to research it well in order to make sure your dog gets a balanced diet. Nor did I want to commit to cooking for Archie because I'm not the sort of person who cooks up batches of food in advance, freezes them, and so on. That's not to say that I haven't cooked food for him in the past, but it's not a long term option, at least not for me. If you choose this option, again you'll have to do your research in order to make sure your dog is getting all the nutrients he needs.

Commercial dog food, for me, is the most convenient option. Archie now has a mix of grain-free kibble and wet food, both from Lily's Kitchen. I did a lot of research on commercial dog food, and I believe that Archie is eating good quality food, with a decent amount of, and decent cuts of, meat in it. He's healthy, his coat is glossy, he's a good weight, so it obviously suits him. Like I said in the first book, do a bit of research and examine the ingredients in your dog's food. What suits one dog won't suit another, so you might have to try different brands, and remember to introduce new food slowly to your dog.

As well as looking at the quality of the food your dog eats, also check out his treats. Some are better than others. If you're UK based I think the treats made by Soopa, Lily's Kitchen, Pooch & Mutt (to name but a few) are good quality, and Archie likes them too!

I mentioned this in *All About Archie*, but it's so important I decided to repeat it here. Keep toxic/harmful food out of the way. Never leave any chocolate lying around. Check for any food you might have dropped on the floor when you're preparing tea, like if you've been chopping onions and some fall on the floor.

I'd also like to flag up xylitol, which is a sugar substitute. If your dog has even a small amount, it could prove fatal. Xylitol can be found in things like peanut butter and chewing gum. If you give your dog peanut butter, check the ingredients, and watch for chewing gum getting stuck on your dog's paws whilst out on a walk. For more information on foods which are toxic for your dog, please check out the Blue Cross for Pets website (see Useful Links).

Sick!

It's horrible when your dog's poorly. He can't tell you what's wrong. I try not to catastrophise – dogs are going to have off days, just like people. If one day Archie's quieter than usual, he usually bounces back quickly.

One day he was sick, bringing up yellow bile. That's happened before, but usually it's a one-off and doesn't occur again for ages, but Archie was sick every few hours. He brought up his food, and even when he fasted for a while he was still bringing up yellow bile. He was playing and seemed happy, if a little quieter, so I tried not to panic.

On the second day he was sick again, so I called the vet's and made an appointment. The vet said this sort of thing is common – Archie probably ate something during a walk which we didn't notice. Archie was given an injection and an anti-acid tablet, along with some Royal Canin Veterinary Diet Recovery food. Archie ate his tea with gusto that evening and we never looked back. No more sickness – hurray!

Archie: *I loved that food. Wish I could eat it all the time. Yum-my!*

Yeast Infection

We saw that Archie was licking his paws more than usual, and later we noticed him scratching his ears a lot. We took him to see the vet and he was diagnosed with a yeast infection. His ears were syringed and we were also given some special anti-bacterial, anti-fungal shampoo called Malaseb, which I was instructed to use on his paws twice a week for three weeks.

We immediately saw a difference in Archie – a lot less scratching and paw-licking. What a relief it must have been for him. We had to see the vet the following week in order for Archie to have his ears syringed a second time, and then again a fortnight later for Archie to be tested again. Thankfully he got the all clear. The vet also gave us some ear drops for him.

Why Archie developed a yeast infection we may never know. There are various causes like allergies, or something getting trapped in your dog's ear. The vet told us that because of his floppy ears, Archie's more prone to a yeast infection. At least we know the signs to look for now. I'll definitely be cleaning his ears more regularly than I used to, and I will continue to use an anti-fungal shampoo on his paws every so often too.

Archie: *I do not, under any circumstances, like having something cold and wet put in my ears! Although – my ears did feel better afterwards. And the more it happens the more I am getting used to it, but ssh! Mum doesn't need to know that. I get treats when she puts the wet stuff in my ears. He he.*

'It's not a journey to embark on if you don't have time and bundles of patience.'

KERRY AND ALFIE

Kerry is mum to one-year-old Shichon, Alfie (he's the same breed as Archie – they're also known as Zuchons). She's had Alfie since he was eight weeks old. Although Alfie is her first family puppy, Kerry herself grew up with Shih Tzus and Border Collies, and she still helps to look after her parents' Border Collies. Here Kerry shares her story, along with some tips on being a puppy parent.

The puppy

When we decided to get a puppy we had to start by researching hypoallergenic breeds, because my youngest stepson is allergic to breeds of dog which shed fur. My husband wanted a small dog so I was excited to see that having a Shih Tzu was an option as I was familiar with the breed, having grown up with them. When we started looking for a litter of puppies we couldn't find any Shih Tzus close by, but then we came across an advert for a litter of Shichons just ten minutes down the road. We felt it was meant to be!

After we had been and chosen Alfie, we spent some time on Google in order to try and gain a better idea of what to expect from our puppy. My parents also bought me a book on Shichons. We brought Alfie home less than two weeks before Christmas, and as we have two young boys at home, it was certainly a very exciting time! It went by in such a whirlwind – I wish I'd kept a diary.

Alfie was very good and would sleep in his crate during the night, although he would always wake early. It was difficult to stay patient with him during toilet training. We thought we'd never get there! At six months old he still seemed to need to pee every twenty minutes, and if we took our eye off the ball there would be another puddle on the floor. Eventually he turned a corner and it clicked with him.

One of my biggest frustrations was that I had wanted a lap dog and to able to have lots of cuddles with my dog, but Alfie wasn't keen on this initially. I'm happy to say that I get plenty of cuddles now!

The teenager
Alfie still has moments when he can be challenging, but I wouldn't change him for the world. Having him as part of our family is amazing, and the thought of him not being around makes me so sad. He has stolen the hearts of everyone in our family.

Kerry's tips for wannabe puppy parents
I would recommend joining breed specific groups online on social networking sites. The participants of such groups are fellow owners and breeders who have experienced the same ups and downs that you will with your puppy. They can offer plentiful advice. I was incredibly lucky to find Jessica, who is the owner of Alfie's sister Ethel, in one of these groups. We keep in touch to compare their progress and share advice. I would really recommend asking your breeder if it's possible to put you in touch with the owners of your puppy's litter mates.

Take your pup to local dog-friendly events and socialise them with other puppies and dogs at every opportunity. We found puppy parties at our local canine crèche, training classes at our local Blue Cross centre, and visits to dog-friendly cafes and parks were great fun. Alfie's socialisation and wellbeing is one of my top priorities, therefore I try to take him with me to as many places as I can. Alfie, like most dogs, loves the beach, so I would recommend finding one where you can take dogs all year round.

If you've already got a puppy and you're struggling …
Don't give up without giving it 100 percent first. If you need help speak to other dog owners, and the breeder if you're able to. Try different techniques if you have persevered with

something and it's not working. Take your puppy to training and socialisation classes, because doing activities together will increase the bond between you.

A final word about Alfie
My husband didn't have pets during his childhood – he's besotted with Alfie. He can't understand why anyone wouldn't want to have a Shichon! Alfie makes us smile every day, and he shows us so much love that I hope we make him happy every day too!

Alfie then and now

Photographs © Kerry Howlett

'Sometimes Archie's poo hangs on because of some hair he's also eaten. We call it "the hanger on", and we have to pull it off for him!'

MUCKY DOG

We were lucky that the woman who used to look after Archie during the day was also training as a dog groomer, so she groomed Archie for us, but when we moved house (over 100 miles away!) we had to look for someone new.

Initially I tried a dog grooming salon. Archie had an appointment towards the end of the day. We took him in and there were some dogs running round, but others were in cages. The woman seemed pleasant enough and Archie went with her quite happily. When we went to pick him up he was running around, just as we'd seen the other dogs when we'd dropped him off earlier. The cut he'd had was fine, but oh, he stank. It wasn't the nice scented smell you expect when you pick your dog up from the groomers, it was more of a strong doggy odour.

When Archie next needed a groom I didn't want to take him back to the salon, partly because of the way he smelt when he came out, but also because of the cages. I searched online and struck gold when I found a woman not too far away from us who did dog grooming at her home (one dog at a time). When I took him to see her she asked me questions about Archie, and took some time to play with him before she started grooming him. I liked that. When I returned, Archie was fine (he looked and smelt good too), and now I think going to see Heather is a treat for Archie. He scampers off with her and does not look back – that always reassures me.

Heather has a Facebook page so I could look up reviews and see pictures. Look for someone like this, or ask around to see if anyone can recommend a groomer.

It's a good idea to either plan to shower yourself once you've washed your dog, or wear a shower cap and some old clothes to protect yourself. If you're not quick enough to shield your dog with a towel as he shakes excess water off, you'll get sprayed and look just as bedraggled as your dog!

Tip: Apply a bit of Vaseline to the hair under your dog's eyes to keep it in place and prevent eyelashes getting in his eyes.

Archie: *When I've had a shower (boo!) I like to run round and then rub my head on all the cushions. I REALLY hate having a wet beard.*

'For the sake of the dog, I'd rather see people educated about it than make an impulsive decision, only to later regret it.'

RENEE AND JAX

Renee McCormick is mum to three-year-old Shichon, Jax (or Jaxson Clyde McCormick to give him his full title). Jax wasn't Renee's first puppy, but he was the first puppy she'd had in a while. Her husband wasn't so keen to get another dog, but Renee persisted! Renee's had Jax since he was nine weeks old. Here she shares her story, along with some tips on being a dog parent.

The puppy
As happy as we were to have Jax, we would get equally frustrated. He didn't pick up on toilet training at all for the first few months. Jax was (and still is) stubborn about some things. It was something we learnt when we researched Shichons. Jax is really smart and picks things up quickly, but we think he's smart enough to decide to do things when he wants to (or not want to, as the case may be).

He cried a lot when he wasn't right next to us, especially at night. We didn't let our other dogs sleep in bed with us, but Jax would cry in his crate even though it was right beside our bed. We put him in his soft carrier crate and placed it between us (we were afraid of rolling on him because he was so tiny!) and he settled. Nowadays he sleeps with us in our bed every night (no more crate). He insists on sleeping right up against one of us or, most of the time, in between my feet!

The adult dog
Jax is my baby boy and he knows it! Just about everything we do revolves around him – I mean that in a good way. He loves to be with us and really likes it when I carry him around. And it doesn't seem like a day goes by when we don't have a conversation about Jax's poo!

33

Life with Jax now is about making sure we do everything to keep him healthy and happy: having him groomed regularly; having the right kind of fruits and veggies on hand to supplement his food; ensuring he has enough play and run time every day; putting toys away each night because it looks like I have young children living in my house; ensuring he has clean water; taking a thousand pictures and videos (just because); making sure he has outfits for special occasions; even giving him little body massages a few times a week.

Jax has settled down with regard to the separation anxiety. He doesn't cry and seem to throw tantrums anymore. And he is so excited to see us – even if he was on his own for just an hour. He still has his moments regarding toileting. We took him to obedience training with a high focus on toilet training. The trainer said he wasn't housebroken, but I now believe that it's not an issue with toilet training, but rather that Jax is marking (even though he's been neutered).

He knows to go to the door when he needs to go out. He has a few spots in the house that he will mark. We have to close doors to certain rooms that he can't be left in alone because chances are, he will mark. He will go weeks without an accident and just when we think we can trust him, he has another accident. If it wasn't for this he would just about be the perfect dog. He gets along with other dogs and is great with people – especially our grandkids.

Renee's tips for wannabe puppy parents
Research, education and patience! I would say the decision to get a puppy, or any pet, needs to be done with a lot of honest thought. It should not be an impulse decision or one taken lightly. Bringing any animal into your life should be a thoughtful decision made knowing you will be caring for a living creature for years. Consider also how your current lifestyle will most likely change – will a dog still fit your lifestyle in five years' time?

I applaud anyone who decides to bring a rescue into their family; however, if an animal is brought into a household without any research, the animal may end up being too much for the owners and returned to the shelter.

If you're looking for a specific breed, do the research and educate yourself. If you're able to, get on sites and/or join groups specific for that breed and ask questions.

Make sure the breeder is ethical and responsible and that they provide a happy and healthy environment for the dogs and puppies. Investigate them to check out their reputation – even visit the facility beforehand. Ask to see the parents and find others who have gone through this breeder.

If you've already got a puppy and you're struggling …
Patience, patience, and more patience. Remember, this is a living creature that is counting on YOU! Know that the puppy will mess up and you might mess up, but you will get out of the experience what you put into it. Invest in your puppy, and I don't just mean financially. Invest your time in teaching them early on.

I highly recommend training classes. If you can't afford something like that, there are numerous books and on-line sites you can go to for training tips and advice. Don't get frustrated and throw in the towel because your hard work will pay off, and it will all be worth it. Remember this is a member of your family and you mean the world to this dog.

A final word about Jax
The first seven months or so were very trying, even after Jax was neutered. Obedience classes have helped a bunch, but I still get frustrated because Jax marks. I know he knows better, but the joy and love that he brings to our home far outweighs my frustration.

Jax then and now

Photographs © Renee McCormick

'It's funny watching Archie dart around in the snow, even funnier to throw a snowball and watch him try to figure out where it's gone!'

SEASONS

Summer

During the summer of 2018, when we had a long-lasting heatwave, we bought Archie a paddling pool, but he wouldn't stay in it when we put in a little bit of water (and I'm talking a really small amount). As I mentioned earlier, it's become an indoor playpen.

I wouldn't recommend spending too much on a paddling pool initially, especially if you're not sure whether your dog is a water baby or not. That said, I definitely wouldn't buy the really thin kind because I'd be wary of my dog's nails ripping the fabric. You could try the plastic kind, but if you do opt for a fabric one, get one that is fairly thick. There are also pools made specifically for dogs.

Archie: *Mum put a little bit of water in my new 'pool', and gave me some treats when I went in it. As soon as the treats stopped I was gone and she couldn't catch me. He he!*

Tips for making sure your pooch keeps cool during the summer:

*Don't take your dog out for a walk during the hottest times of the day – try to go early morning and/or late evening.

*If your route involves walking on pavements, to avoid your dog burning his paws place your hand on the pavement. If it's too uncomfortable for you to keep your hand in place for at least five seconds, then it's too hot for your dog to walk on.

*Always have plenty of water with you. There are special water bottles available for dogs, along with collapsible water bowls. I've bought a simple child's flask for Archie – he's small enough to drink from the cup.

*Hopefully you already know this but I don't think it does any harm to emphasise it: NEVER EVER leave your dog in the car on a hot day, not even for a few minutes. And I would avoid too much car travel in general in hot weather.

*Don't let your dog overexert himself. If your dog likes water then swimming would be great exercise on a hot day, but if not, get out those puzzle toys. There are toys you can buy which can be filled with water and frozen, or even put in some treats, peanut butter, mashed banana, and again, freeze. The options are endless.

*If your dog enjoys lying in the garden, ensure he's in a shady spot, and keep an eye on him. Have a bowl of water available outside too.

*Some dogs like being sprayed by the hose (Archie doesn't, but some of his pals at day care love it).

*I soaked a microfibre towel for Archie for him to lie on. He wouldn't lie on it (or on a cool mat), so I draped it over his back.

*I bought a ceramic bowl for Archie's water because it helps to keep his water cooler for longer.

*Try throwing some frozen peas or carrots or blueberries (any safe fruit or veg, basically) for your dog to search for.

Archie sleeps in our bedroom and when the clocks went forward, he started waking us up earlier and earlier, so we bought a blackout blind. It was worth the money because now we get to sleep in a bit later.

Winter
The winter of 2017/18 was a harsher one than we'd experienced for many years. I certainly saw more snow than I ever had when we were living down South. Although Archie had seen snow, it was only ever a thin smattering and melted away within a few hours. In Shropshire we had huge dollops of the white stuff, which took days to clear.

I didn't realise that snow would create more work in terms of cleaning Archie up after a walk. The snow got caught up in his hair – he had mini ice-balls all over his legs! It didn't brush out, so we took to showering him in lukewarm water (as we would have anyway to clean his paws), but it took a little longer to thaw the ice-balls. It was getting to be a pain though, showering every time he went out in the garden, so I bought him a fleece all-in-one from Etsy. It's easy to get on and off (unlike another suit I tried), and does a good job of covering his legs. And guess what? I got to test it out before publishing this book because it snowed!

At first Archie looked unsure, and I wondered if he would even move in it. This has happened before with coats – if he doesn't like the feel of something he won't budge! But to my surprise he went out, did his business, and even ran round. And when he came in he just had a bit of snow on the bottom of his legs which came off with a quick towel rub and he didn't need a shower. Result! Even if it just helps to keep the snow off him when he goes out in the garden it will have done its job.

During the winter months I became worried about Archie getting too cold at night. I was going to buy him a heat pad, but when I did some research I was concerned about his safety (leakage, wires, zips to chew and so on, depending upon the type of pad bought). I like making things and so I thought I'd make him something similar to what humans use for aches and pains – a heat pad you can gently warm in the microwave.

Mine is filled with oat flakes because I thought if Archie was to chew it, he probably wouldn't be interested in oat flakes and even if he was, they wouldn't do him any harm. Also, they give off a nice smell when the pad is heated up.

The oat flakes are inside a sealed cotton cover, and the fleecy outer cover is made out of Archie's old puppy blanket. It has no zips, but it's removable and therefore washable. Very simple and quick to make, and it's something warm I can put in Archie's basket on colder nights. He even uses it during the warmer months (not heated, of course), because it's a little pillow for him to put his head on.

Anti-freeze poisoning and rock salt poisoning could make your dog very ill (in some cases it may prove fatal). Prevention is key. Don't allow your dog to drink from puddles, and after winter walks always rinse your dog's paws thoroughly.

If you've got anti-freeze at home ensure it's stored in a safe place, clean up any spills immediately, dispose of the bottle safely, and make sure your dog isn't around when you're topping up your car radiator (check also that your car radiator isn't leaking). If you suspect your dog has ingested either anti-freeze or rock salt, consult a vet IMMEDIATELY.

'How dare people try to steal dogs in order to make money out of them? It makes me so angry. Dogs are much-loved family members.'

SECURITY MATTERS

It's scary – the amount of lost or stolen dog reports I see now on social media. It's one of my biggest fears – that someone will try to take Archie – and I can't believe that in the eyes of the law (UK) dog theft is not viewed any differently to that of inanimate objects. The theft of a dog – a much loved member of the family – will have a devastating effect on its human family.

What can we do to keep our dogs safe?
*Ensure your dog has a collar and tag with your contact details on it. I put my contact details on the tag, but left Archie's name off. I know some people have their dog's name engraved on the tag. I think that if someone's trying to take your dog and they can see what his name is, it could make it easier for them to get closer to him. It's worth just bearing in mind.

*Make sure your contact details are up to date for your dog's microchip.

*Never EVER leave your dog unattended in the car because a thief could try to break in and take your dog whilst you're shopping, nor outside a shop because a dog tied to a post is ripe for stealing, and not even in your own garden unless it's fully enclosed with high fences. Check the gates are locked. Even then I would suggest always keeping an eye on your dog. Now that we've moved, Archie's got a larger garden to run around in but the gate is near a main road, so I always keep Archie in sight in case someone stops, leans over the gate and tries to take him. All it would take is me popping inside for a minute.

*Be mindful that someone could attempt to snatch your dog whilst you're out on a walk. I'm not scaremongering, I'm sure the risk is very low, but I've heard stories ... Awareness is key. Keep your dog on a lead and keep a good grip on that lead – maybe loop it round your wrist more than once. We've got an extendable lead with a plastic handle, so we can't do that, but my husband attached some elastic to the handle, which we put round our wrists. Try to keep to public areas and don't always use the same route; vary the times you go for a walk.

I never let Archie off his lead during a walk, anyway, because he hasn't got a reliable recall as yet. I use an extendable lead so he has some freedom, but he can be reeled in, if needs be. Perhaps it's no bad thing, as a dog off the lead can go on ahead of its owner and is more of a target for thieves (equally the dog could get lost).

*Be wary of anyone expressing too much interest in your dog's breed, how much he cost, and so on.

You've heard my side of things, and all of the contributors to this book (except Archie) are female. I thought it would be useful to get a man's point of view and so I asked my husband, Simon, for his take on bringing up a puppy – our Archie.

'I thought having a dog would be like having a cat, but with the addition of taking it for a walk. How wrong I was.'

A MAN AND HIS DOG

You didn't want a dog for years. What changed your mind?
I thought a dog would be a great addition to the household and give my wife and me something to focus our attention and energy on.

How did you feel when you first met Archie?
I couldn't believe how small he was, being only eight weeks old. I thought we couldn't visit the breeder and say no, leaving him there. He was a tiny, vulnerable animal in need of a home.

How did you feel the day you brought Archie home?
Excited and nervous.

What were the early days like?
Terrible. The excitement quickly wore off and then the stress began.

What was the lowest point?
About three days after getting him and feeling like we'd made a mistake; it was overwhelming the amount of time and energy needed to look after a new puppy. We spent most of the time cleaning sloppy poo and wee off a carpet that had

never had so much as a glass of water spilt on it before Archie's arrival.

What made you keep going?

The thought that if we took him back to the breeder, or found another home for him, I would feel like the worst human being ever to have walked the earth.

What helped?

People who had been through the experience also recalling how bad it was and telling us that things would get better.

When did things start getting easier?

When he was toilet-trained several months later. When he did his first poo outside it was one of the best days of my life. Also when we could finally stop putting newspaper down in the hall overnight.

What is life like now with Archie?

Busy; he's still young so needs one or two walks a day and playtime. He needs almost constant human contact and even sleeps on the bed. It's very hard work, which I find stressful at times. But there are other times when it feels good, like when you return home and he goes bonkers when he sees you.

What would you say to anyone thinking about getting a puppy?

Stop and think hard. Do you really know what you are letting yourself in for? When Archie was a puppy, several people I spoke to told me that, in their opinion, having a puppy was harder than having a baby.

Archie: *Dad shares his sausages with me even when he doesn't really want to.*

'Archie's such a character, and it's a privilege to have him in my life.'

It often feels like life revolves around Archie, and for the most part that's okay. There are still some days when I wish I was curled up on the sofa reading a good book rather than having to battle the elements to take Archie out for a walk, or dealing with sick, or washing muddy paws, or trying to prevent Archie from eating poo (and, worse, being licked by Archie after he's eaten the said poo), or being sprayed with fluid when Archie shakes himself after I've just inserted drops into his ears. I could go on, but I'm sure you get the picture.

Archie's a much loved member of our family, and yet sometimes it's nice to have a break from him, like when he goes to his nana's or to doggy day care. Everyone needs time out. Some dogs are more independent than others, but Archie is a dog who always wants to be by my side, even when I'm trying to meditate!

Puppies are demanding to be sure, and adult dogs also need a lot of attention. It's not like having a hamster – a dog needs exercise and mental stimulation every single day (oh, and lots and lots of love, which is the easy part).

I read something about having babies, which applies to dogs too – that you have to *really really* want one in order to do a half decent job, because it's tough. Don't get distracted by the cute factor. Do lots of research and take your time, because it isn't a decision to be taken lightly.

But enough of the doom and gloom. I have no regrets where Archie's concerned. Yes, it's been hard at times, and I do wish I'd been more prepared for the impact he'd have on my life, but that's all in the past. In the present, nothing beats having a cuddle with Archie, or seeing his little face alight with joy when he's running after his ball. When he dives on the sofa and rolls around on his back, messing up the throws and cushions in the process, he makes me laugh.

Right, now I believe Archie wants to have a word, so I'll hand you over. Thanks for reading!

Love from Helen and Archie x

Archie: *That's all lovely, Mum, but I want to know why I can't dig on the sofa. It's one of my favourite things to do.*

PS. You know you said I'll be banned from the new sofa when you get one? Yeah right, like that's ever going to happen. Love and licks!

Some feedback that I received from the first book was how much people enjoyed reading Archie's comments, so I thought it would be fun to let him tell the story of our summer road trip in 2017, when we sold our house, put all our belongings into storage, and travelled round various parts of the UK, before finally settling down in Shropshire.

THE ADVENTURES OF ARCHIE ZUCHON – ROAD TRIP!

Mum says we're going on an ad-ven-ture. I don't know what ad-ven-ture means, only that it involves the car. I didn't used to like the car, but now I know it means I get to go all sorts of places.

I wish I could sit on Mum's lap in the front of the car, but she says I can't and that I must be secured (it's something called the L-A-W), so I sit in the back. I have the whole seat to myself, which is good, I can stretch out.

Back to our ad-ven-ture. Our first stop is a place called Appleby. I'm thinking we'll see lots of apples. I don't like apples – Mum's tried giving me a small piece from time to time – but I do like peas and carrots!

When I first get out of the car I can't see any apples, but the smells are a-maz-ing. The place we're staying in has a strange garden that I must explore straight away. Never mind unpacking, Mum! There isn't any grass, just some potted plants. What's that all about? I don't mind going inside when Dad comes back with sausage and chips. He's bought an extra sausage just for me. I love my dad. A treat, Mum says. Yum yum. Appleby's all right by me!

I'm not sure how long we stay for – time means nothing to me – and I confess to feeling a little homesick, but I soon forget because we go to lots of different places. I can't remember all the names. I can tell you all about the smells, though. He he. Mum's relieved it doesn't rain, which is something of a mi-ra-cle in this area, apparently. I get loads of attention from the humans, and I see lots of other dogs.

Mum says she's never seen so many dog-friendly places. I, of course, think we dogs should be allowed to go everywhere humans go (although I can take or leave a clothes shop; like dad, like dog).

One thing – I do wish the humans wouldn't pat my head when they first meet me. We dogs don't like that. We'd much prefer to sniff your hand first, and a stroke on the side would be lovely, thank you very much.

I get another sausage in Bowness-on-Windermere. Result! And in Pooley Bridge, where I'm allowed INSIDE the restaurant, there are comfy beds especially for dogs, as well as bowls of water. I'm impressed. Mum slips me some of her chicken dinner. I love my mum.

It almost seems a shame to leave Cumbria (although I'm not fussed on the lakes themselves – I'm no water baby), but leave we must, so Mum and Dad say. It's an ad-ven-ture, remember. On to the Scottish Highlands – it'll be my very first time in Scotland.

This time around the place we're staying at has lots of grass, a whole mountain range, in fact. I'm not quite sure what to make of it. There is what Mum calls a loch (a funny name for just another lake) close by. It doesn't impress me!

Ooh, but the smells are a-maz-ing. There's heather – at least I think that's what it's called. The sun seems to shine for ages up here, and even at night it doesn't go completely dark, which is good for us when the electricity goes off. Dad's in his element and goes out to gaze at the stars, but I think Mum's a bit freaked out, though she's trying not to show it. She's much happier when the lights come back on.

You know the best bit about being away from home? I get to sleep with Mum and Dad. At home I wasn't allowed in their bedroom and I slept in the hall (boo!). They tried the same set-up when we reached Appleby, but I wasn't having any of it. I can cry all night, you know – put me to the test and I'll show you. Dad always breaks first. Surprised? I'm not. He's a softie, really.

I see deer and Highland cows (Mum says I remind her of a mini version of one of those because my hair has grown and my fringe is rather cool, though I do say so myself), but don't talk to me about midgies. Ugh! They're everywhere.

I can't say I'm impressed with the sausages up here either. They're cooked in batter for some reason. Why spoil a good thing?

Mum and Dad take me to my first beach, a place called Cromarty. The pale gold stuff – sand, is it? – feels nice under my paws. Shame Mum won't let me dig. She tries to get me to dip my paws in the sea, but I'm not having any of it.

We go to Loch Ness, too. I won't paddle and that's not because I'm scared Nessie will pop out at me. It's too windy for me, and I decide I don't want to walk, so Dad has to carry me all the way back to the car. He he.

Dad's a bit grumpy in Aviemore because of all the tourists, but he cheers up when we're in the Cairngorm Mountains. It's really windy, so Mum stays in the car, but Dad takes me for a little walk. I'm pleased when we get back in the car. Oh, and guess what? Mum and Dad have some lunch at the Speyside Heather Centre, and I see a red squirrel! Dad takes a photo of it. I want to go and introduce myself, but Mum and Dad won't let me. Boo!

At the end of the week we move south, to Stirlingshire. We're staying in the grounds of an old castle and we're surrounded by fields. Mum gets excited when she sees lots of lambs. I wonder if they'd like to play?

One day, when we're out on a walk, Mum and Dad notice there's a bird of prey circling above us. Dad's worried it's going to swoop down and make a grab for me (I'm a bit worried too), so he picks me up and carries me back to the cottage. Ahh! I love my dad.

Mum looks on something called the in-ter-net and finds us a great place to eat in Call-en-dar. The café's upstairs and it has a special section for dogs (and their humans, of course), complete with beds, bowls of water, and biscuits too. Result!

Some of the staff come over to see me specially. I love, love, love this place!

Ooh – you know I told you we went to Loch Ness? Mum and Dad decide I have to see Loch Lomond since we're in the area. And guess what? I have my first paddle. I'm not sure at first, but Mum stays with me, encouraging me. I love my mum. The water's very low, and well, I quite like it. I'm not sure about getting any more than my paws wet. I'll have to think about that.

Next we go to stay near a place called Ayr. It's a place as new for Mum and Dad as it is for me, so we're all exploring. My nana calls us the three musketeers! I like Ayr. Mum and Dad do, too, as we often go down to the sea front and look across to the Isle of Arran. Mum takes me on the beach, but I don't go for a paddle as the sea always seems to be far out whenever we go. I think it's for the best as I still haven't made my mind up about how far to go in next time. I do find some giant puddles though; no, not puddles, rock pools, I think Dad calls them.

We find another nice café in Troon where the nice lady brings me a bowl of water and a treat. Mum is doing a great job finding these places. Dad wants a haircut and spies a barber's. I bark when he leaves us, but Mum takes me to the promenade and I forget all about Dad. She lifts me up so I can see over the wall. Hmm … That's a lot of water. Mum seems nice and chilled, though, and says what a lovely day it is. I guess the sea is okay – over there!

Another day we venture into the Galloway Forest Park and see Loch Doon, which Dad says was where a gunnery school was set up during the First World War. I'm not sure what that means. It's raining – Mum doesn't like the rain and doesn't want me getting wet – so we get back in the car and wait for Dad. He's busy taking pictures of the ruins of a castle. I can't say I see the appeal. Yawn.

We're all sad leaving Ayr. On our last day we go to the beach again. Mum has a fishcake supper, whilst Dad has a sausage supper. Can you guess which one I prefer? He he. I made some friends here. Three La-bra-dors have been staying next door to us – each a different colour – one golden, one black, and one red. Did you know I used to have red hair? Mum's a redhead and she said we used to match! But my hair has faded now.

Anyway, even though they're all bigger than me I can hold my own, and I'm sorry to be saying goodbye to them. Maybe we'll meet again someday.

We're heading south now, leaving Scotland and heading down to somewhere called Shropshire. It's still light when we arrive and I'm so glad to stretch my legs (even though Mum and Dad stopped lots of times along the way). The place we're staying in has a back garden overlooking hills – the Shropshire Hills, apparently. Mum and Dad enjoy watching the sun set, whilst I'm de-light-ed to find a dead bird, and immediately investigate it. Mum shrieks, Dad quickly removes the bird (boo!) and we all go back inside.

We go to this really cool place called Bridgnorth, which has a cliff railway. I stare at it for ages. And in Much Wenlock we find yet more cafes where I'm allowed in. Result! We doggies are taking over the world.

Because we're not too far from North Wales, Mum and Dad take me to see my granddog parents and my auntie. I get loads of attention (and sausages) so I'm happy.

Then Mum and Dad decide to revisit some old haunts so we go the scenic route through Llangollen, past Llyn Celyn, where my hair is blown all over the place. I don't like it. Eventually we get to Betws something or other where it's very busy and Dad gets grumpy. He feels better when he's had some lunch (me too). And the day isn't over. We drive past Snowdon, where we stop for Dad to take pics. I look up as far as I can, but my neck's too short and so I can't see the peak. We eventually make it to Conwy where I really like watching the boats. I also like the piece of burger Mum gives me. I love my mum!

We explore more of Shropshire, even venturing into Shrewsbury one day. On Dad's birthday we go to another part of Wales, this time in Powys, to Llyn Vyrnwy. Have I spelt that right, Mum? Yes. Good-oh. Lake, loch, llyn, they're all the same to me. You're allowed to walk across the dam, but I can't see a thing, so Dad lifts me up so I can see over the wall (I love my dad) and then I wish he hadn't because I see all that water.

Our ad-ven-ture is nearly over as Mum and Dad have decided to stop travelling and have found us a lovely cottage in the country. I have mixed feelings about this. I have love, love, loved seeing so many new places. I've been to England, Scotland and Wales. But I think it's nice to know my bed's going to be in one place for a while. Mum and Dad take me there to have a look and I love the garden – it's massive; lots of exploring to do. A squirrel, a grey one this time, runs right past me. The cheek!

All in all, it's been a blast, but I'm looking forward to my new ad-ven-ture now.

Licks,

Archie

ARCHIE PHOTOGRAPHS

Here are some of my favourite photographs of Archie. They were taken during the last twelve months, apart from the last two, which were taken during Archie's ad-ven-tures in the summer of 2017.

Photographs © Helen Edwards and Simon Edwards

USEFUL LINKS

https://www.anxietyuk.org.uk/get-help/anxiety-uk-national-infoline-service/

https://www.anxietyuk.org.uk/blog/my-puppy-anxiety/

https://www.bluecross.org.uk/pet-advice/basic-first-aid-dogs

https://www.bluecross.org.uk/pet-advice/foods-poisonous-dogs

https://www.facebook.com/groups/canineenrichment/

https://www.facebook.com/groups/311758695982183/ (New Puppy and Dog Owners Advice and Support Group)

https://www.facebook.com/groups/shihtzubichonshichon/

https://www.industripet.com/product/lickimat-playdate/

http://pickpocketforagers.com/

https://www.thehonestkitchen.com/blog/diy-make-your-dog-or-cat-a-snuffle-matt/

The section on Christmas has appeared in two web articles – here are the links:

https://spoiledhounds.com/puppy-for-christmas-present/

https://dogsmonthly.co.uk/2019/01/25/why-christmas-isnt-the-best-time-to-get-a-puppy/

ACKNOWLEDGEMENTS

I would like to take this opportunity to thank the contributors to this book, Kerry Howlett, Renee McCormick, Kath Pearce, Rachel Radtke, and Bryony Yates. Your input has been invaluable – thank you.

Thanks to Anne Hamilton of WriteRight Editing for helping to make this book into the best version it could be.

Thank you to Helen Pryke for proofreading this book. Your attention to detail is amazing!

A big thank you to all the supporters of the first book, *All About Archie: Bringing Up A Puppy*. A special mention must go to Karen Loughran. I'm so chuffed that my book has become part of your puppy pack.

Thanks to everyone who has helped us on our journey so far with Archie. I'd also like to mention canine behaviourist, trainer and author, Kate Mallatrat, who provided me with discounted PickPocket Fabric Food Foragers.

Thanks to my husband, Simon, for your contribution to this book and for another great cover.

And to Archie – thank you for being in my life and for inspiring me to write two books. Here's to many more years together, and who knows? Maybe another book.

ABOUT THE AUTHOR

Helen was born in North Wales and she currently lives in Shropshire with her husband, Simon, and her Zuchon dog, Archie. She has always loved writing stories, ever since she wrote a short story collection in the style of Enid Blyton when she was 12. After working for many years in the public sector, Helen took the plunge to become a full-time freelance writer. She loves the Scottish Highlands, crisps, pizza, reading, taking photographs, and anything sparkly.

To find out more about Helen and Archie please go to:
Blog www.helenlibbywriter.blogspot.com
Facebook www.facebook.com/ArchieZuchon/
Instagram @helibedw
Pinterest www.pinterest.co.uk/helibedw
Twitter @helibedw

Also by Helen Edwards

All About Archie: Bringing Up A Puppy

Are you a wannabe puppy parent? Have you just brought home your furry friend and are feeling overwhelmed, anxious, or just plain exhausted? You're not alone.

There's no doubt your new best friend is going to be cute, funny, loveable, and hard work!

In this book Helen shares her experience of bringing up her puppy, Archie, because knowing what to expect is half the battle.

Available in eBook, paperback and audiobook format from Amazon.

Audiobook also available via audible and iTunes.

Paperback also available from Nantwich Bookshop!

59253424R00033

Made in the USA
Columbia, SC
01 June 2019